Active Innovation

ACTIVE INNOVATION:

EXERCISES IN
PROBLEM SOLVING AND INNOVATION
2ND EDITION

DR. RYAN VAN ZEE AND TERESA QUINN, M.ED.

Table of Contents

OVERVIEW

The following section will give you insight to why we do what we do when we teach innovation. As authors of an innovation textbook, and professors of innovation, we have dedicated ourselves to understanding the process of students learning innovation. We have learned that innovation is not innovation until it is implemented. An unimplemented innovation is an idea that does not actually belong to you. Only an implemented innovation belongs to you. This misunderstanding is the largest obstacle for our students to understand.

We have used the principles of this textbook in one form or another for over a decade. Through all our experiences and surprises we know that every student can innovate with success. Of course the success is related to the student's effort.

About This Textbook

This book was written with the principle that innovation is occurring all the time, within us and around us. Even the smallest change is innovation. Innovation is not necessarily invention, but has more to do with changes to existing products and services.

What makes this innovation textbook unique? The process of *innovation phases* presented in this textbook are not specific to any academic or professional discipline. This textbook focuses on the student's unique interests and background knowledge rather than content from his/her academic major. We believe this personalized and open-ended model of learning is the best way to foster innovation in students.

Similarly, this textbook is **not** designed to increase knowledge in a content major, but to apply critical thinking and problem-solving skills through exercises and activities that produce innovation. The corresponding course is an application-based class, with much less emphasis on content, and much more emphasis on your interests and abilities. The phases of innovation focus on the problem-solving process for innovation. This problem-solving approach directs you to think deliberately and divergently, and to gain the skills required to innovate. Innovation terms are included in this textbook to help you build your knowledge of how and when the innovation process occurs.

All examples in this textbook are student-tested exercises and activities which engage the student's interest to innovate. The included exercises interest and engage students at various levels. This aligns with the process of innovation – no two people are the same and innovation does not occur at a steady pace. The exercises are meant for the student to build upon, and to support the development of an innovation through intrinsic motivation, not just for getting a good grade.

Above all, it is critical that the student choose his/her own identified problem to bring to the innovation process, and it does not need to be connected to her/his major. Research shows that intrinsically motivated individuals have the highest percentage of successful innovation. However, the process of innovative thinking can also be applied to an academic major/discipline to produce a discipline-related innovation.

However, current college curriculum which emphasizes innovation implementation is based upon the student's field of study or major. Although, the student is interested in that field of study, or major, not everyone in that field of study is interested in the same problems or topics. Therefore, major-specific innovation tends to be individualistic and/or be a task for a grade, not for the betterment of self and others. Intrinsic motivation rules a successful innovation.

● ●

There are some very basic **phases of innovation – identification**, **ideation**, and **implementation**. You will learn how these three phases work to produce innovation. This textbook is **not** intended to help you design and build the "flying car." This textbook is designed to direct you to develop the basic skills of innovation. An idea might come to you in a burst of excitement, or you may have already asked yourself several "What if....?" questions, but it is the process of developing the ideas to implementation that results in innovation.

The exercises within the three phases are based on student-tested experiences. Examples given throughout the textbook are actual student outcomes. The innovation phases can be changed to accommodate your innovation, but it is not recommended that you omit any phase in the process since you may lose direct or indirect insights for developing your innovation.

There are several activities in this textbook that will help you narrow your focus so you can innovate to your fullest potential. In the Appendix of this textbook are basic examples of each exercise or activity. Each exercise or activity example is a recent student example.

■■

Our society celebrates fresh **ideas**. We do not profess this to be undeserving. However, an idea is not an innovation or problem-solving. All ideas are just ideas. We believe that idea generation is important in the innovation process, but ideas are not innovations.

Innovation derives from a need. We encourage you to disengage from *invention* for invention's sake, and to think about *change*. In our classes, we illustrate this point by saying, "Don't try to invent the flying car," but to incrementally change your way of thinking. Also, try not to impress people with something novel in order to be celebrated, but try to change lives by helping people in new ways.

During the first part of this course you are given a framework of innovation: identification, ideation, and implementation. Identification and ideation tend to go rather smoothly; however, implementation is not as easy. Do not choose the most attractive or impressive idea, but instead pick an idea that you have intrinsic motivation to work on and that you can implement in real-time. Manageability is key. Along the innovation journey you will learn crisis-management, time-management, communications, and collaboration.

This textbook was designed to help you produce two different innovations. These innovations will be produced consecutively. The first innovation is created with little direction – do not be alarmed. The first innovation is known as the **$5 Innovation**. The *$5 innovation*, with the hands-off approach, is to help you and your professor gauge your understanding of innovation. The second innovation, or *The Active Innovation*, encompasses several exercises and activities to advance your innovation. The exercises and activities engage many resources that were not required in the *$5 Innovation*.

The skills developed through *The Active Innovation* will help you as you move from education to professional life. Many students implemented innovations that were simple in execution, but they created a base of knowledge to cultivate a new way of thinking. This new way of thinking will be your go-to approach as problem/needs/issues surface in your professional life.

■■

CHAPTER 1 -
Innovation and Problem-Solving

Innovation – the development of a product, service, or cause that is new, or a bit different. It can be as far-reaching in application as global use, or as local as community service. The intended outcome, however, is for the betterment of more than one user. Innovation is rooted in continuous motivation to improve upon an existing innovation. In other words, the innovation will evolve as more users are identified for its benefit.

Problem-Solving is different than innovation. Problem-solving, for this textbook's purposes, is intended to remedy a problem for the individual and/or to reach a pre-determined goal (like completing a puzzle). Whereas innovation is the remedy to a problem without a determined end point that will help many people.

Innovation example

> *I have a plot of land that is not being used by me, but it costs me money. I want to discover a solution to maintain the land so I am no longer losing money.*

You can look at the land as a type of product. If someone is willing to rent the land from you, that person can be seen as an example of the "market." Once you are doing business it is a **product market fit** if it is successful.

If you design an innovation as a *product market fit*, you will help others. To further explain, if the land is used to board horses for cross-country travelers, the travelers will pay the owner, but all the travelers now have a place to board her horses during a cross-country journey. The owner has to consider how to accommodate the travelers and the horses and many other steps, but the purpose of the land has been changed. The products and services added to the land are the implementation of the innovation.

You may say that **entrepreneurship** is at work here, and not innovation. However, we disagree – we believe it is both. The land accommodations are changed which is a requirement of innovation – change. The change in the use of the land to boarding accommodations is the innovation. To meet the product/market fit, fences will need to be built, shelter erected, and water made accessible. If the land is left as is--a big open space--horse owners will not board their horses on the land because the horse is not secure. From there a business is built. The innovation in regard to the land will affect and benefit the landowner and others. However, if the land was not used in a business, but say a garden, if would be problem-solving. This is the synergy of innovation.

■■■

Problem-Solving is to fix a problem for the individual. This could be a problem of yours or someone else. It may appear that solving a problem for someone else would meet the definition of innovation, however, it is not. The problem being fixed for another does not affect you, long-term. However, if you were to take the information you received from the solved-problem and implemented it as a replicable fix, then it is an innovation. This distinction may be like splitting hairs, but hair-splitting is needed with innovation.

Problem-solving example

> *I like to garden. I need to find a place on my land where I can start a garden.*

This is solving a problem. The problem is not designed to help others. It is not to say that the solved problem will not help others, but that is not the initial intent. Once the problem is solved to your liking or reaches the defined goal, the process is complete.

■■

The "Aha Moment" and Innovation Genius

"Aha Moment"

The "**aha moment**" is the moment when an idea hits you. An "aha moment" is a combination of all your conscious and subconscious processing coming together. It could just come to you in an instance with no seemingly rational explanation for its existence (like in the shower), or you could have been working on it for a while. As you continue in this textbook, you will come to understand there are many avenues to understand the "aha moment."

There might be questions why the "aha moment" is listed in the innovation and problem-solving section. The reason for this question is that an "aha moment" is the generation of an idea. However, sometimes, innovation flows from an "aha moment," and sometimes the "aha moment" is unrelated. The "aha moment" is referred to as an ideation, which is the second phase of the innovation process.

Innovation genius

Geniuses do not create the most practical, everyday innovations. There is a never-ending flow of innovation, but a rather limited number of geniuses. Although geniuses are of superior intellect, they are people, too. A genius may be able to produce a more elaborate innovation, but the motivation for innovating can be matched by those of regular intelligence.

Therefore, you do not have to be a genius to be innovative. Innovation stems from a need to solve a problem, not genius.

■ ■

Other Innovation Tidbits

Thinking differently as opposed to thinking deliberately

A wise man once said, "To tell someone to think differently is as helpful to would-be innovators as 'swing differently' is to golfers" (Razeghi, 2008, p. 6). When you tell someone to think differently about a situation, what are you really telling that person? Nothing. "Think differently" is a useless statement to someone who needs guidance. However, to tell someone to think deliberately, you are at least giving some direction. To think deliberately about a situation, thoughts become focused on the situation in need of change. There are no answers in "Think deliberately," however, the focus is put on the problem and that is a good place to start.

Failure

Just the mention of the word **failure** is painful. Innovation is not an idea; it is a tangible outcome which produces a product, service, or cause, when fully implemented. Since innovation requires a new or different tangible outcome, there's often a struggle with implementation, and early failure is likely. *Fortunately*, failure is inevitable. Sad, but true; failure is one of the most indispensable events to any success. It is hard to have an appreciation for failure because it is no fun. However, failure sharpens us; it sharpens our minds and provides the energy needed to make success a reality.

As an example, failure can be due to the lack of implementation. Listing "steps" to implement is not "proof" of *future* implementation. Ideas are not innovations, and innovations are not "correct." Innovations must be implemented.

CHAPTER 2 -

Understanding the Concepts and Innovation Terms

Concepts of Innovation

The **concepts of innovation** were identified to give labels to events which happen during the innovation process. The process of innovation is within every one of us. Innovation requires active engagement with the concepts and active guidance. Learning to spell is not an innate skill, but a nurtured skill. A human's ability to innovate is innate; however, the systematic skills process is learned. The benefit to mastering the process of innovation is that it can be applied to known and unknown future challenges.

The basics concepts of the innovation process include **connections, constraints, resources, intrinsic and extrinsic motivatio**n, and **sleep**.

Sometimes, connections are not obvious. To understand connections is to understand that all things are connected, and to better understand the world in which we exist. The problem is that many of these connections are not obvious, and thus go unrecognized for some time. We should try to discover some of these connections to better our state of affairs, and to innovate. Some connections are simple, while others take weeks to think through. Since innovation is not a predetermined outcome, we must discover how solutions to other problems can be applied in new ways. If this principle is practiced, connections help us see possible answers.

■ ■

Constraints of Innovation

Constraints- while many of us don't like the idea of being constrained in one way or other, we are. It is because of constraints that innovation is required. No one is asked to fix something that works perfectly. Instead of having constraints work against us, we can creatively devise strategies to have these constraints work for us. Time constraints, for example, may be seen as a negative stressor; however, most of us realize if it wasn't for the last minute, nothing would ever get done. While not having enough money can be rough, it can get the innovative juices flowing about how to save more money, how to improve your chances for a promotion, or how to start a viable business.

"Curiosity is the mother of invention" is a helpful, but not an all-encompassing cliché of innovation. It is constraints that makes us dig deeper into our abilities. Determine which constraint is holding you back as you pursue a solution, then alter the way you manage and use the constraint.

Behavioral	Human Obstacles	Fear Energy Cognitive	Physical Biological Emotional
Resources	Material Limitation	Time Money Materials	Tangible

Constraints Matrix

Related to the grid above, let's say there is a lack of capital, or money, for your innovation. The lack of capital is the **resource constraint**. If you have an intended innovation that requires money, yet you have none, you need **not** stop. It is the presence of the money constraint that will add more creativity and problem-solving to the innovation process and phases. You will determine how to solve the problem without additional capital. Buying something would have been the easy fix; your fix will be outside the norm.

■ ■

Motivation and Innovation

According to researchers in the field of motivation, **Richard Ryan** and **Edward Deci**, **motivation** means to be moved by something – either intrinsically (internally), or extrinsically (external). If you have no inspiration to act, you will be characterized as unmotivated. Being unmotivated has negative societal consequences and hurts innovation.

Intrinsic and Extrinsic Motivation Examples

Money is an external motivation. Initially, you might disagree with this statement. Some may say they only care about money, and can only think about making mountains of it, thus, it must be an intrinsic motivation. Unless you enjoy holding money, and not spending it, money is extrinsic. It is the things that you can do with money that is intrinsic, and that is what needs to be identified.

Here is an example of the difference between external and internal motivation. Your high school teacher may have informed your parents you were unmotivated in her class, and therefore, characterized you as a low preforming student. In high school, classes are specific. One class is about math, one is about English, and so forth. Thus, a creative writer might struggle in math. Furthermore, your grades might be the only evidence your teacher uses to judge your motivation. But, if you were to think back on that situation, it was not that you are a low preforming individual, but that you had lower intrinsic motivation toward math than English.

You may be curious of the classmates that were also creative writers and complained endlessly about their lack of interest in math, but earned considerably higher grades in math than you. Your teacher may even point to this fact to solidify that you are a low-performing individual compared to your peers. However, the difference could be motivation. The student that hated math as much as you, and openly complained that math would never help her in her career as a writer, might have relied on an extrinsic motivation that pushed her to focus on math.

Is there a particular college she wants to get in, and a low math grade would hinder that acceptance? Is there a reward system in place at home by her parents which grants more leisure time? Or is there another external motivator that promotes good math grades when otherwise math is of no interest to the student?

Let's review the factors in this case. Your classmate lacks intrinsic motivation for math. **Intrinsic motivation**, means to act upon something because it is inherently interesting or enjoyable to you. Consider the options for external motivation in your friend's life. **Extrinsic motivation**, refers to doing something because it leads to a distinguishable outcome. Consider asking people about their hidden or unexpected motivators to better understand human behavior. The more you know about motivation, the more you can prepare an innovation that people will use.

Consider what motivates you – intrinsically and extrinsically. In the boxes below, list a few things in each.

Motivation Exercise

Your Intrinsic Motivators

Your Extrinsic Motivators

Intrinsic motivation is the core of innovation.

∙∙∙

Sleep and Innovation

Ironically, **sleep** is one of the most powerful tools in the field of innovation. Sleep is a naturally recurring state of mind and body. Changes to the mind and body during sleep to support innovation are an altered consciousness, uninhibited sensory activity, and reduced interactions with surroundings. Our brains do not shut off while sleeping, on the contrary, many researchers believe the brain is more active in the ability to solve problems while the body rests. This makes sense in the fact that the brain must keep functioning to maintain life, but is able to divert processing from daily survival to subconscious issues. When awake, we are bombarded with excessive stimuli. Research overwhelmingly supports the continuous processing of relevant and seemingly unrelated events during sleep. In other words, we are free to make creative connections because we are relaxed, free of judgment, and not distracted by day-to-day life.

Our brains are, by their very nature, designed to solve problems. If we query our own brain before we go to sleep, it will start devising a strategy to solve that problem both consciously and unconsciously. Research on test-takers which study the night before a test, then obtain a good night's sleep, continually reported higher test scores opposed to those that "pulled all-nighters." Also, research supports the benefits of sleep on physical health. A study conducted on runners showed there was an identified decrease in performance after just one night of sleep deprivation.

Give this sleep exercise a try:

> Before you go to sleep, focus lightly on a problem. Do not try to solve the problem before you go to sleep. Do not think too far in-depth about the problem to make yourself anxious. If you feel there is benefit in jotting some notes down before you go to sleep, do so.
>
> This exercise is not to add more work to your day. This exercise is designed to decrease the imbalance of problem-solving. Review your problem immediately when you awake. What happened? If

you insist nothing happened, think about the problem later in the day or keep trying the sleep strategy for a few days in a row. The results of others have proved very successful.

Sleep exercise

Jot down your experience with your sleep exercise in these boxes:

Problem	Outcome

••

Innovation Resources

Resources are the people, places, and things you have access to. Everyone has resources. Resources are distributed based on who we are. Some resources can be controlled, and some cannot.

What some people struggle with is identifying their resources. Money tends to be the focus of many. Many resources have a monetary value, but many valuable resources are free.

Here are a few free resources:

> **Friends and family:** family and friends bring a host of resources, from knowledge to skills. As an example, a student wanted to develop an app to connect students with campus events. He had no

idea how to make an app. He was talking to a friend one evening, and come to find out, the friend made apps all the time!

Age: Being in a certain age group gives added knowledge and access to that age group.

Geographical location: Where, and to some extent, how you live is a resource. Even the most remote location offers resources that heavily populated places will not have access to.

Skills: Can you think critically, strategize, organize? Your knowledge and ability within skill sets is a resource. Even when you do not have paints and canvas, you still have the skills required to paint. How else might those skills be applied?

Most people don't realize that their most needed resources are knowledge and a strategy. What kind of resources do you have access to?

Resource exercise

List an Inventory of your resources:

Jot down some of the resources *YOU possess* here:

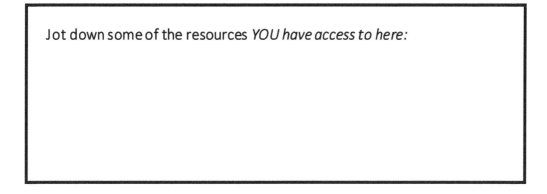

Jot down some of the resources *YOU have access to here:*

Innovation Terms

The following is a list of additional terms you will use in this textbook.

Communication – is a necessary information gathering tool for innovation. As noted in the definition of innovation, an innovation must help yourself and others. Without regularly communicating with the "others," there is no way you can meet their needs or receive feedback on trial runs of your innovation.

Additionally, communication with seemingly unrelated actors in your environment leads to robust innovation development. Communication experts say the biggest barrier in meaningful communication is that the individual spends more time preparing for what they want to say, without listening closely enough to the other person. This naturally causes a disconnect from presentation to response. If innovation communication intends to produce a final outcome, that helps yourself and others, listening and responding based on others will get you there more efficiently.

Collaboration – collaboration consists of input to the innovation between the innovator and the end-user. Collaboration can also mean working with a like-minded innovator. As an example, two students were concerned with dorm living health – one was concerned with food; one was concerned with exercise. By working together, they could build on important aspects that were of use to two innovations.

Confluence Model of Creativity – a model of insight paired with knowledge. Insights derive from the senses, the way one thinks, one's personality, and environmental factors. Basically, it is all the small factors that come together at once to make a new connection.

Copy and tweak – means taking an existing product or service and changing it to make it your own. Innovation is the outcome of a change and most of the time an innovation is not a brand-new invention. Also realize that when you come up with what you think is a "brand new invention," the "brand new invention" is built with your previous knowledge of existing products and services. To fast-track innovation, consider copying an idea and tweaking it to make it your own to produce a completely new use for an existing product or service.

Convergent thinking - the ability to give the "correct" answer to standardized questions. The process does not require creativity and is appropriate thinking for procedural tasks. An example of convergent thinking is solving a crossword puzzle or multiple-choice testing.

Creative Code – a creative code is a unique set of activities that set your strategy of regularly engaging in innovation development. When you need to create something new, or even just solve a problem, a creative code is your way of working through the process.

Since none of us go about this process in the same way, sometimes a creative code is hard to identify or point out. When we begin engaging our creative code, none of us know exactly the various steps in our process as it is naturally occurring in us – don't fight it. We call this a code because we have to crack it for ourselves through trial and error. We all have a supply of creativity and we can implement that creativity if we discover how. Our unique code cannot be replicated by another individual.

Divergent thinking – a thought process or method used to generate creative ideas by exploring many possible solutions. An example of divergent thinking is innovation since there is no predetermined correct answer.

Feedback – feedback for innovation should be designed for continuous improvement. In other words, receiving advice that is substantive in nature is more useful. Gathering feedback can be direct or indirect. **Direct feedback** is a process in which the innovator solicits input on the innovation, like a survey. **Indirect feedback** is received by observation of your surroundings and making connections to your innovation.

Ideation – is the middle part of innovation. Ideation means thinking of as many possible solutions to the problem as possible – Brainstorming!

The ideation part of innovation is understood through the "**left and right brain" theory.** Although the brain consists of two hemispheres, scientist do not truly believe the brain works in two independent sections. The "left brain, right brain theory" means there are two types of thinking.

Left-brain activity is considered organized and logical, and the functions include:
- logic
- sequencing
- linear thinking
- mathematics
- facts
- thinking in words

Right-brain activity is more visual and intuitive. It has a more creative and less organized way of thinking.
- imagination
- holistic thinking
- intuition
- arts
- rhythm

- nonverbal cues
- feelings visualization
- daydreaming

Once a problem has been identified as worthwhile, the left-brain theory needs to engage in the work of coming up with a multitude of solutions which need to be written down. The left-brain part of innovation is logical and sequential. Once an extensive list has been complied, it is time to engage the right-brain process. The right-brain process will include several distinctions that come from intuition.

Identification of a problem – problem identification is where the entire process of innovation starts. The problem you identify must be meaningful to you and affect other people. As a rational person with limited amounts of time, you should abandon problems that are not supported by your intrinsic motivation. Since innovation is a difficult process that takes time, you should only engage in problems that are worthwhile to you. Identifying the right problem is a problem in and of itself, but is an essential step. Any problem identified is the beginning of worthwhile work. If your motivation for the innovation is based on intrinsic motivation, the innovation process will retain value well beyond college.

Implementation – implementation is the most critical aspect of innovation. Implementation is the difference between an idea and an innovation. There is a saying in innovation that goes like this…*if you know what to do and you know how to do it, go ahead and do it.* Give it a try and find out how other people use your innovation in expected and unexpected ways.

If you know what the problem is and have ideated the solution, you must put it into play to be an innovation, otherwise, it is just an idea. Another way to process the difference between an idea and an innovation is that an innovation is the outcome that can be critiqued by your users.

Innovation – innovation is a higher form of problem-solving. Innovation is systematic and replicable so it is a unique solution for more than one person. An innovation is a product, service, or social cause that brings about change for multiple persons. Innovation is not necessarily the same as invention.

Left-brain, right brain theory - the "left brain, right brain theory" means there are two types of thinking. Left brain is logical; right brain is creative. (More on left brain, right brain theory can be found under ideation.)

Looping – looping, in innovation, is not failure. Looping is completely contrary to failure. Looping back and starting over at a previous data point is highly progressive. If your innovation goes off course, or worse, crashes, you need to loop back around to the point before you got off track. When you return to that point, then you are miles ahead of where you were the first time because you have eliminated one or more possible solutions. You are closer to developing the right solution.

Open-ended questions – an open-ended question is an avenue for an innovator to gather feedback during the innovation process. *Yes*-or-*no* questions give little to go on for the process of development. An open-ended question requires the answer to give meaningful feedback. An open-ended question does not always need to come from the innovator. The end-user should ask the innovator open-ended questions to help the process.

Painfully obvious - every question you know the answer to is easy; and every question you don't know the answer to is hard. There are many things that look complicated and hard to understand until you understand them. Sound obvious doesn't it? However, when you try and try to figure something out, it is painfully obvious when the answer is revealed. The notion of something being painfully obvious becomes a running joke in the field of innovation. Paper that sticks on the wall without needing tape? Genius/obvious.

Philosophers and innovation – early philosophers eluded to the concepts of innovation and the human condition. **Aristotle** believed we should "think about thinking." **Thomas Aquinas**, a Dominican priest and Scriptural theologian, referred to a part of the gospels that is useful in understanding how we operate as informed actors. The gospels refer to "loving God with all your heart, all your will, all your soul, all your mind, and all your strength." Aquinas believed our soul is at the top of this list. He went on to say the mind is the actor of the soul; the mind can determine where to put the will. This is also known as the heart of action. Our mind's choice puts the will to work to get what the mind desires. Our intentionality can determine what we become.

Pivot – pivoting is one of the most useful tools in your innovation toolbox. Pivoting in innovation means to change course. Changing the innovation process after research, information, or knowledge can make the original innovation undesirable to pursue. The change in course can be a complete scrap of your original innovation, or a drastic change to your existing innovation. Pivoting is a hyper-tweak.

Having the knowledge that a pivot is a natural process of innovation allows you to get away from the false notion that you need to be right the first time. You may be tempted to stay the course with a struggling innovation because the amount of time you have invested will be wasted. However, this notion is false. The more you try to shove a square peg into a round hole is time that is completely wasted. The more pushing and shoving to prove you are right – even though you are not – is just plain stubbornness, and a negative influence upon the magic of innovation.

Problem-solving – is not innovation. Problem-solving solves a problem for the individual who has the problem, whereas innovation solves a problem for the individual and others. If you find that the solved problem only helps you, you are not innovating. However, problem-solving assists in developing strategies, like solving puzzles, that are tests of the mind. Problem-solving is a useful practice for building the skills for innovation.

Product market fit – product market fit means to find a product that satisfies the need of a market. A product market fit, while certainly seen as a business term, is much more than that. Another way to look at product market fit is to think of a *product* as your solution, a market as your user that has the problem, and the fit is the innovation.

Race to the bottom is one of the issues early innovators are tempted by. The race to the bottom is the temptation to take the easy way out. This race is won by the student that announces early on that he/she has no ability to understand the material. This race to the bottom is inspired by simple thinking. In this race, the simpler the better. Innovation, and the related skills required, do not support the easy way out.

Let's say you had to convince your professor that you simply cannot understand the concepts. The race to the bottom is won by not trying or caring. You simply must care to even begin to think about the innovation process. Having no passion will win the race to the bottom. Don't be that person. Professors know you are not; most of your classmates know you are not (the ones that are not easily fooled). Therefore, you are only fooling yourself.

Social innovation – there is really not much difference between social innovation and innovation except the direct intent. When your direct intent is intentionally pointed at a social cause, this is often referred to as social innovation. A social innovation, is a new, or a bit different approach to a problem which enhances a social group's cause.

As an example, a student was sick of the college food. Her parents regularly sent her care-packages with food. However, this college student could only handle so many boxes of macaroni and cheese. Her floor-mate received a care-package from her parents, too. In her pack were endless cans of tomato soup. The student with the mac and cheese implemented an innovation that helped her and her dorm. It was a give-one-get-one dorm food bank. If the students partnered with the local food bank to serve the hungry in their community, they would have moved from solving a problem of not enough food variety to a social innovation that got college students involved in the mission of the local food bank.

Scale – is the process of growth. When working with your innovation, it is often useful to start over to better understand what you are working on. Once you start having some success, then you are ready for growth. Scaling includes the steps involved when implementing your innovation for a larger audience.

Statements – stating a thought usually lacks discernable value to the innovator. A statement is just information without clarity.

An example of a statement that lacks value – "I don't like it." The only way a statement like this will continue is if the innovator follows up the statement with an open-ended question. What is it that you do not like? If the innovator was unskilled at open-ended questions, he/she could think the entire innovation is unlikable, as opposed to something else. Maybe the end-user just didn't like the color.

Thinking deliberately – thinking deliberately is thinking in a specific way, and requires someone to pay deliberate attention to thoughts and unrelated events. Thinking deliberately is a dedicated time of thinking about the problem.

Thinking differently - thinking differently is telling someone to do something without instructions: "to tell someone to think differently is as helpful to would-be innovators as 'swing differently' is to golfers."

Tweak – to tweak an innovation is slightly different than copy and tweak. A tweak is a slight change in your process of innovation. It is a smaller change than a pivot.

CHAPTER 3 –

The State of Innovation

Organizational and Workforce Demands

There is a strong consensus that innovation is a necessary requirement of today's workforce. **Innovation** is a "new idea, object, or practice that is created, developed or reinvented for the first time in an organization" (Walker, 2014). Without innovation, organizations become disadvantaged, not only in their industry, but also globally.

Research conducted by The **Association of American Colleges and Universities** (AACU) identified what current employers are looking for in new college graduates in terms of innovative thinking, and what they perceive they are receiving. The research indicated that 95% of employers surveyed prefer college graduates to contribute to the workplace with innovative thinking. Furthermore, nine in ten employers agreed that innovation is essential for future organizational success and growth. Additionally, employers surveyed (93%) are less concerned with a graduate's major, and were more interested in the graduate's ability to communicate effectively and to solve complex problems.

Motivation and Workplace Innovation

Daniel Pink, an expert in motivation, has compared motivational techniques of the industrial era with today. According to Pink's research, today's employers are looking for individuals who can contribute across department lines, as opposed to the industrial era of specific task assignment. Pink's rejection of the notion that all employees can be given a problem, and equally apply motivation to solve the problem, supports the AACU's, research findings. Furthermore, Pink describes that most organization's innovative and money-making ideas have come from an employee's ability to apply his/her own intrinsic value to an autonomous project of the employee's choice.

Some organizational leaders have recognized this process, and have implemented autonomous worktime, similar to the "15%-time" of 3M back in the 1940s. The **15%-time** concept was designed to allow individuals 15% of their work week to create and innovate on projects that had intrinsic value to them. This *15%-time* produced the universally known innovation of *Post-It Notes* by 3M. Today, well-known organizations are adopting this old-yet-new concept to increase the production of money-making innovations.

Additionally, research strongly suggests rewards systems are changing in today's workplace. The industrial era supported *if/then* rewards in the workplace. **If/then** rewards are...*if the prescribed tasked is completed to expectations, then a reward will be given. If/then* employee rewards to nurture innovative thinking pale in comparison to the autonomous and intrinsic work reward system.

The *if/then* reward system, from the Industrial Era, can be observed in traditional task-based school projects. As an example, *if* a good project is presented, *then* a good grade will be rewarded. However, the process provides little in actual innovation learning, intrinsic motivation, or divergent thinking because the goal is a reward – a good grade- for completing a task.

Today's organizations are beginning to embrace the old-yet-new methodology of intrinsic motivation rewards to foster innovation. Several prominent organizations are eager to offer creative workspace for the development of intrinsically-motivated innovation. However, employers have expressed concern for the lack of cross-disciplinary innovative-thinking college graduates bring to the workforce. Therefore, the time is right for this type of pedagogy in higher education.

Higher Education and Innovation

Even with innovation becoming a field in and of itself in some higher education institutions, one main struggle exists. The struggle exists between developing robust innovation college curriculum with students from the American K-12 **Common Core** era. Common Core Standards and standardized testing teaching practices in the United States are based on convergent thinking, and innovation is based on divergent thinking. **Convergent thinking**, a term developed by **Joy Paul Guilford**, means the ability to determine the correct answer to a multiple-choice question, leaving little to no room for creativity. There is no correct answer in innovation, just implementation.

Divergent thinking, on the other hand, "refers to that strategy of solving problems characterized by the proposal of a multiplicity of possible solutions in an attempt to determine the one that works" (Idea generation: Divergent vs. convergent thinking, 2015, para. 2). This method of teaching has been diminished in today's K-12 education system. There is no "correct" answer in divergent thinking, just answers that work.

As colleges and universities embrace innovation, the dismantling of the programmed mindset of the entering college freshmen is daunting. The learning process from convergent thinking to divergent thinking has posed more challenges than expected.

College Curriculum and Innovation

Currently, there are three college-level innovation teaching approaches most commonly found in the literature. The first approach is when the student is in his/her discipline, using that discipline's curriculum to solve a discipline-related problem. Within this structure, deliverables can be graded and assessed to measure the student's learning process.

27

However, to accomplish this type of assessment, the deliverable must be related to the field. This process is actually problem-solving since the outcome is usually the student's grade. Once the problem is solved, the process is abandoned. This assignment-centered approach almost completely eliminates the intrinsic motivation processes. The whole point of intrinsically motivated innovations is that it cannot be dictated by any external demand – it must be unique to the individual student.

This first approach to teaching innovation can be an effective problem-solving teaching method. With assignments like case studies, essays, proposals, and presentations, students are learning to think creatively related to their field of study, with appropriate assessments. This approach works well for content knowledge acquisition, analysis, and synthesis, but it lacks the cross-organizational, or cross-disciplinary innovative thinking skills desired by today's workforce where employees solve real problems for their customers.

The second approach is when students are taken outside their discipline, and required to innovate a solution to a problem in a discipline they know little to nothing about. It is often the professor's expertise that is informing this structure, and serves to provide a measure for implementation. Students of all majors can be assembled in one class together, but it is the appropriate major-specific deliverables that are determined and evaluated by the instructor.

This approach clearly misses the intrinsic motivation aspect of innovation. As an example, in a research study of non-graphic design students placed in a course with a graphics design instructor, they were instructed to innovate a graphic design project. Since the students were not graphic designers, the outcomes were not intrinsic, but they were creative and solved a problem. Whether the problem was to receive a grade, or to finish a project, the problem was solved, yet innovation did not happen.

Both teaching scenarios are currently considered limited in replicating real-world innovation job skills. Yes, organizations need skill-specific tasks brought to completion with discipline-related education, but it is the cross-organizational innovations today's organizations are searching for. Bringing a directive to completion is task completion and practices several skills, but is not innovation.

The third approach is connected to invention and **STEM majors (science, technology, engineering or mathematics)**. STEM courses promote a variance of intrinsic motivated innovation *inventions*. For example, build a structure out of the supplied popsicle sticks that can support a ten-pound weight. However, invention in the context of cross-organizational contributions tends to stay within the STEM departments.

Furthermore, research cites the growing concern of global issues such as climate change, human rights, and healthcare are less likely to be solved with invention, and will be better served by intrinsically-motivated social innovation.

Therefore, a college curriculum struggles to identify and produce cross-disciplinary innovative results. It is difficult and expensive, especially for smaller universities, to assemble a class of mixed majors, cross-discipline students to innovate based purely on intrinsic-valued projects.

In review, the four contributing factors which have been identified as barriers to efficiently teaching innovative thinking skills, regardless of a student's major, when all other identified teaching methods are negated, are:

(a) the student is past freshman-level classes, and the student is somewhat programed to produce results within his/her chosen major;

(b) instructors are experts in particular disciplines, making them easily influenced to assess and grade based on their particular field of study;

(c) the lack of assessment tools for mixed disciplinary innovative projects; and

(d) the resources to allocate funds for strictly intrinsic motivation innovation classes.

A fully functional cross-disciplinary innovation course must remove the barrier of major, yet provide assessment of progression in innovation. This combination will be found in this course.

What's next?

This textbook is designed to jump start you, your class or your entire institution in the intrinsic learning of innovation! There are several exercises that were designed to pry you away from traditional learning and get you innovating.

The premise of this book and the development of this curriculum is that students are required to choose a problem that is unique to them and without regard for major. This approach aligns with the theory of intrinsic motivation and autonomous learning as the student will be engaged and motivated to produce an innovation.

The approach in this textbook, and the skills it will develop will help your professional prospects. There is an increasing employment barrier for recent college graduates in regards to the rapidly changing demands of today's modern organizations. Organizations look to colleges to graduate students who can assimilate into the new work culture of required innovative thinking and implemented outcomes.

It is the requirement of most organizations to maintain a technological edge, as well as address needs of the global market. Gone are the times when skilled employees were assigned a task and judged based on execution of that task. The shift to promote autonomy of employees to innovate projects, problems, and ideas of their own has proved profitable for organizations. This textbook is directly addressing concerns students have about the relevance of their education. For the purpose of this textbook, the skills you learn are more important than the specific content you learn.

Closing Thoughts on the State of Innovation

In conclusion, there is a disconnect between what employers are looking for cross-disciplinary, innovative thinkers and how colleges are teaching innovation. In the United States, standardized testing is predominant in the K-12 sector of education, causing concern for real-world application and adaptability. The two kinds of problem-solving that support education are (a) convergent thinking; and (b) divergent thinking. Convergent thinking is prevalent in K-12 in that the educational process strives for one correct answer to a problem. Divergent thinking requires multiple outcomes. With convergent thinking, innovative thinking is stifled, only allowing for specific outcomes. Divergent thinking supports the assertion that autonomous thinking supports innovation. While using this curriculum, keep in mind that there is no correct answer, just implemented innovations!

This curriculum is designed and tested to produce innovative thinkers.

CHAPTER 4 -

Innovation Framework

Fill Your Bucket to the Brim

Although this book is designed for you to intrinsically innovate, it is important to have a context from which to start. Through experience, it has been determined that the following four "**buckets**" are the framework of almost all innovation. These *buckets* are the platform for you to build your innovation. Your family, career, friends, beliefs, etc. can be put into one or more of these buckets to help you focus. The buckets are **health, faith, education, and business.**

Some of your buckets may hold two of the same value, and some buckets may be fuller than others. This is a representation of you, so you set the value and there are no wrong answers. Remember to think about connections, especially those that are not obvious.

As an example on how to fill your buckets - a student-athlete loved to braid hair. She would braid some of her teammate's hair before every game. When asked which bucket she would put that in she said "faith." She tried to explain her reasoning to the class, but it seemed to only make sense to her...and that is ok...they are your buckets!

In the following exercise you will fill your buckets. In each bucket, list some type of interest, skill, or hobby that you would like to expand upon that relate to that bucket. Here are some examples to help you decide the framework of your bucket.

The following diagram is an example of filled buckets.

Buckets

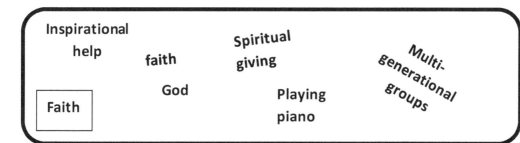

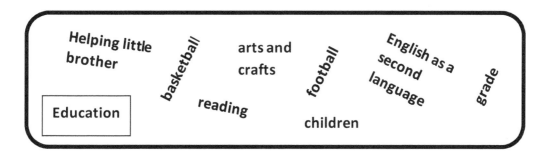

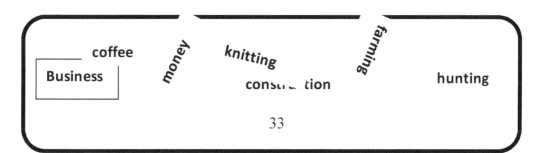

Fill your bucket(s). Jot down your **interests, hobbies, and skills** within a relevant bucket. Not all buckets need to be equally filled, and some of your interests, hobbies, and skills might be in more than one bucket. The connection might only make sense to you.

Health

Faith

Education

Business

CHAPTER 5 -
The $5 Innovation
Let's Get Innovating!

The $5 Innovation

The objective of the $5 Innovation is to overcome the fear of implementing an idea. Innovation is not ideas. Ideas are ideas. Innovation is the ability to implement an idea into a tangible outcome. There are three **components to innovation**: (1) identification; (2) ideation; and (3) implementation.

Many people equate innovation with technology or invention. Technology is an influential part of innovation, but it is not the basis. Innovation is extracted from a need - a need of self and others.

The most simplistic innovation devoid of technology can solve a problem as well as an innovation developed exclusively with technology. What an innovation comes down to is intrinsic motivation. Then, with available resources the innovation comes to life. With a $5 limit you probably can't rely on much technology for your innovation.

It is understood that this process might feel overwhelming. Undue social pressure produces a mindset that big is best, and that to produce something magnificent is to have generated value. When thinking about innovation, one usually thinks of what is deemed to be grand – Apple Inc.,

Tesla, and NASA. But in actuality, it is everyday innovations that make magnificent differences in our life.

Always keep in mind these two principles of innovation:
1. An innovation must be implemented
2. An innovation must help yourself and others

Here are two examples of a $5 Innovation. One is a service and one is a product. Both are fixing a problem of self and others.

Service:
> You are a nurse. You work in a busy private practice office for two general practitioners. You are responsible for calling patients in from the waiting room, directing the patients to the exam room, taking vitals and collecting and recording general visit information.
>
> Often the doctors get behind and patients must wait an extended period of time. Many of your patients are elderly and become sore and stiff from sitting for long periods. When the elderly patients are called back, you are their first contact. Many of the elderly patients who waited for a long period of time are upset because they are now uncomfortable. To make matters worse, they are unable to participate fully for you because of their discomfort, and you can't accurately take their vitals. The need to remedy this problem is for you and the patients. You are unable to properly do your job, and the patients are very uncomfortable.
>
> After speaking with the elderly patients, you realize it is the chairs – they are not suited for the elderly. You do some quick research online and find ergonomic padding for the chairs to help the elderly. You know your doctors will not replace all the chairs in the waiting room, but you think they would buy affordable padding. With the few, you could make a "senior section" designed for the elderly. The senior section would also have other amenities specific to the elderly. You speak with some of your patients to try out the

accommodation. You present it to the doctors, they approve, and you implement.

Product:

The other example is the current broom/dustpan combo. Your dorm floor is linoleum. You are constantly sweeping the floor. The thin line of remaining dirt drives you nuts, and you spend more time trying to pick up the line of dirt than you do sweeping the whole room. Additionally, your roommate doesn't even bother to pick up the leftover line of dirt...he just leaves it. You both want a clean room. You decide to make an attached product (copy and tweak). It is a length of sticky tape similar to what you find on Post-It Notes and lint brushes. You attach it to the bottom of the dustpan. You have your roommate try it out. He gives you a few suggestions and you now have an innovation. This did not cost more than a pad of sticky notes and your room is clean!

The $5 Innovation

The **$5 Innovation** is to get you started with innovation. Do not over think this first innovation. The purpose of this innovation is to help you and your instructor gain knowledge of your level of understanding of innovation. However, this is not a test. Again, do not overthink!

Instructions for the $5 Innovation:

You must not spend more than $5 for this innovation. There are three exercises that will help you frame your problem into an innovation. The three exercises are: Bug Report, Focus Report, and the Ideate Grid. Instructions will accommodate the exercises.

1. Your budget is $5. You don't have to spend any money, but if you do, do not spend more than $5!

2. Review the phases of innovation.
    a. Consider your intrinsic motivators.
    b. Identification of the problem.
    c. Ideate solutions to the problem.
    d. Implement a tangible innovation.

3. Fill out the required exercise sheets.

4. Produce an innovation.

Reminders:

An innovation helps you and others. If the outcome only helps you, then it is problem-solving.

Innovations are the best when they are based upon intrinsic motivation.

Technology is not necessary for an innovation.

Don't overthink!

Have a little fun with your Bugs!

The Bug Report Overview

The **Bug Report** is a warm-up exercise to help you reflect on needs, problems, issues, or "bugs" that have meaning to you. As mentioned, the intrinsic value felt by the innovator leads to the best innovations. When filling out the Bug Report, expand your general thinking. An innovation must help you and others, thus a "bug" which is only relevant to you is not the most productive use of the report.

Bad Example - Bug: 8 a.m. classes   **Solution:** Sleep in
Good Example - Bug: slow lines at the coffee shop   **Solution:** pre-order app

As you are filling out the Bug Report, reflect on Bugs in terms that a person could actually implement as a solution to that Bug. This reflection does not necessarily mean you have the skills or resources to make it happen, but do the skills exist? Is your solution realistic? Such as…your Bug might be that you dislike bullies. A solution derived from technology, skills, or resources that do not exist shouldn't be brainstormed as a solution. As an example with bullies - *use brain control of the bully to make them stop*. That is not a good use of this exercise. However, resources do exist to make a school-wide anti-bullying campaign. You may not have the resources at this time, but it could happen in the future. You may not know exactly how to develop a unique and successful campaign, yet, but that's for a later step.

Instructions for the Bug Report:

1. List 15 things that "bug" you. Try to stay away from things that are too abstract, such as pollution.

2. Write 15 corresponding solutions that you could **implement**.

    - **Example Bug 1:** It bugs me that headphone wires get tangled.
    - **Example solution**: Color code wires for easy detangling.

    - **Example Bug 2:** It bugs me that there are long lines at lunch.
    - **Example solution:** Develop an "order ahead" app at the school cafeteria.

Bug Report

Bug	Solution
1	
2	
3	
4	
5	
6	
7	
8	
9	
10	
11	
12	
13	
14	
15	

Focus Report

Time to focus! Select five Bugs from your Bug Report that you would like to explore for possible innovations. The **Focus Report** will help you narrow your innovation. Write a Bug in its own box, then EXPAND possible solutions for each Bug in each box. ***Rank in order of preference.***

Remember an innovation is not an innovation unless it is implemented. If your possible solutions are not implementable, rework them.

Rank

Bug:
Possible solution:

Bug:
Possible solution:

Bug:
Possible solution:

Bug:
Possible solution:

Bug:
Possible solution:

Ideate Grid

The **Ideate Grid** will help you ideate five solutions to your favorite Bug and help you identify a possible combination from the Focus Report.

Ideate Grid Instructions:

1. Write your top ranked Bug and possible solution from your Focus Report in the top box.
2. List five solutions you could implement to make it happen.

Pick your favorite Bug:

1.

2.

3.

4.

5.

Implementation Presentation

Select one or a combination of solutions from your Ideate Grid to implement. Keep in mind the title of this section...**implementation**. An innovation must be implemented to be an innovation. Insisting that you "Would do it if you had the time or money," or "All my friends think it's a good idea," is not implementation.

Prepare and present your innovation to your class after you have implemented it.

Implementation Presentation Instructions:

Create a 5 – 7 slide Keynote presentation or 2-3 minute iMovie
1. Include your identified problem.
2. Steps taken to innovate.
3. Final outcome of innovation.
    a. props, and prototypes to help show implementation.

After your presentation:

Now that you have completed the $5 Innovation, reflect. Do you feel you have a grasp of innovation? If the answer is no, there is nothing to worry about. Innovation is a continuous process. Although you may feel you did not learn how to innovate, you learned a lot that can be applied. Keep an open mind for the next innovation.

Peer Evaluation

People enhance their ability to innovate with peer interaction. Listening to presentations is not a passive experience. Listen to the innovation presentations of your peers and provide three suggestions or alternatives to improve the innovation. Use the following form for peer feedback. After your classmate's presentation, send a message to the presenter that includes your feedback.

Presenter's Name:

Your Name:

Innovation presented:

I like the fact that...

I wonder if...

A good next step might
be...

CHAPTER 6 -
The Active Innovation

The Active Innovation

The $5 Innovation was a trail innovation, so to speak. The exercises encouraged forward thinking, but at the same time, did not expect you to grasp all the concepts of innovation. If you felt you struggled, relax, and reset for Innovation 2 – *The Active Innovation*.

This is your second innovation. With *Active Innovation*, try to stay focused on the activity at hand. Do not try to force an innovation. The three phases in the Active Innovation model help guide a more engaging innovation. Go through the phases of the Active Innovation with an open mind, and see where your ideas take you.

There are three phases in **The Active Innovation**. The phases are **identification** (of the problem), **ideation**, and **implementation**. These phases were designed to help you produce your most authentic innovation - one that will affect your life and the lives of others.

Good Luck!

Phase 1

Identification

Of Your Active Innovation

Bucket Refill

Problem Statement

Root Cause

Identification

Identification of the problem is where the entire process of innovation starts. The problem you identify must be meaningful to you and affect other people. As a rational person with limited time you should pursue problems you are intrinsically motivated to solve. Since innovation is a difficult process that takes time, you should only engage in solutions that are worth pursuing.

Identifying the right problem to solve is a problem in and of itself, but is an essential step. Identifying the problem is the beginning of worthwhile work. If your motivation for the innovation is based on your intrinsic motivation, the innovation process will have value beyond college.

Bucket Refill – Identification Exercise #1

Let's refill your buckets. Now that you have a better understanding of buckets in relation to innovation, list your ideas with greater confidence that you could cause improvements than last time.

Bucket Refill

Health

Faith

Education

Business

Problem Statement - Identification Exercise #2

The Problem Statement exercise is designed to help you identify a problem to work towards a solution, or an innovation. The Problem Statement is different from the Bug Report as it is not intended to state a solution. It is the first part of the innovation process.

Here are a few tips that should keep you on the right track. Again, an innovation helps you and others, therefore, your problem statement must be in line with that premise.

- **Focus on one problem**
- **One to two sentences long**
- **Must not contain a solution**
- **Must be ambiguous**
- **Must be devoid of assumptions**

Instructions for Problem Statement:

1. State your *where you are and where you want to be,* then work through the three questions of each section on *"Does and Does Not Affect."*
2. Restate the problem with the new insights.
3. Then combine the two to make one new *Problem Statement.*
4. That will be the new problem statement for the next activities in this textbook.

This is an exercise to make you think. It will start out confusing, but it will make more sense the more you think about it. Don't just "get it done"; think it through until it makes sense.

An example of this exercise can be found in the Appendix.

Problem Statement

State where you are:	State where you want to be:

Does Affect	Does Affect
Who?	Who?
What?	What?
Why?	Why?

Does Not Affect	Does Not Affect
Who?	Who?
What?	What?
Why?	Why?

Restate	Restate

Combine the two restates to make a *Problem Statement*

Root Cause – Problem Identification Exercise #3

The root cause of a situation is the drilled-down intrinsic motivator. The best way to determine your intrinsic motivator, or root cause, is to ask yourself five why questions. Each "Why?" builds from the previous answer. After you answer a "why," rephrase the answer into a question that questions your last answer. Do not deviate from your previous answer to write the next question, simply take the answer and rephrase into your next question.

Root Cause – 5 Motivating Whys Instructions:

1. Write your final problem statement from the previous exercise – The Problem Statement – at the top of the *Root Cause – 5 Motivating Whys* exercise.
2. Ask five *why* questions that pertain to your motivation.
3. **DO NOT INCLUDE SOLUTIONS IN YOUR ANSWER. FOCUS ON MOTIVATION**.
4. Answer the *why* question before moving onto the next *why* question.
5. The final box should identify your root cause, or intrinsic motivation.

An example of this exercise can be found in the Appendix.

Root Cause - 5 Motivating Whys

Write you final problem from your Problem Statement here:
Why? Answer:
Why? Answer:
Why? Answer:
Why? Answer:
Why? Answer:
Root Cause (Motivation):

Phase 2
Ideation

Of Your Active Innovation

Pod Development

Combined Ideation

Value Proposition

Input – Advisory Board and Meeting

Looping

SMARTER Goals

Action Plan

Ideation

Ideation is the act of identifying many possible solutions to your identified problem. In this section you will work on exercises that will increase your bank of potential solutions. By far, the ideation phase of any innovation is the most labor intensive and time-consuming. However, this is not busy work. This work will help you innovate as best as you possibly can. There are nine exercises in this section which feed off each other. Work deliberately!

The **Pod Development** exercise can generate what seems like random or silly outcomes. You may even be tempted to get silly in your solutions. That is all part of the process.

As an example, one student thought he was running out of possible solutions in the Pod Development for his identified problem of wasting paper. He decided to write down "make paper airplanes" as one of his possible solutions. Laughing it off, he thought he was free. But one of his classmates had a different idea. His classmate was new to the school and wanted to make new friends. He wanted to start activities to keep students entertained. Yep, you guessed it...paper airplane races!

The moral to the story is don't overthink! Have fun with your solutions, you never know what might happen!

The **Combined Ideation** exercise will seem a bit confusing at first. However, it is in the creative ideation section, so let your mind go free. You will randomly circle three solutions from the Pod Development exercise and list them in the first section of the Combined Ideation exercise. Then, combine those three solutions to make a new solution. Repeat four times. This exercise will produce solutions that were inspired by your intuition or gut instinct.

The **Value Proposition** exercise is next. A value proposition identifies what you believe to be true about your innovation. **Simon Sinek's** TedTalk from 2009 states the difference between an organization's success with and without a value proposition. Sinek keenly presents obvious failures of large organizations that did not identify what they believe.

The **Advisory Board** is a list of five people that will give you valuable and useful input to your innovation. It is important to have variety and diversity on your board. For this exercise, at least one professor is required to be on your board. Which professor to choose for your advisory board will be identified from your *Buckets*. Your other advisors can be anyone with the skills or knowledge to help you.

You will gather your advisory board for an **advisory board meeting**. The meeting is to gain insights and knowledge from your advisory board. After your meeting you will review your notes and decide how your loop should work – pivot or scale.

SMARTER Goals are goals that are designed to keep you focused on what you are doing and what it means to you.

The **Action Plan** exercise will help you get off the couch and to start innovating. Without organizing which steps need to be completed, you could potentially feel overwhelmed and confused on what to do next. The Action Plan exercise requires you to think through your next steps.

Pod Development - Ideation Exercise #1

This exercise will take at least *an hour* to complete because you will need to pause in order to think of additional ideas. Give yourself the time. Don't rush the solutions. *Don't overthink!* Have fun.

There is a total of 5 worksheet exercises in all which will produce **24 possible solutions** to your identified problem (as determined in the Root Cause exercise). A solution is **not** an outcome, but a way you can address and innovate a solution to your identified problem.

Pod Development Exercise Instructions:

1. Complete the Level 1 Pod Development with your identified problem from the Root Cause exercise in the middle box. Each of the surrounding boxes are for solutions.
2. Write one possible solution to your identified problem in each of the four boxes around the identified problem: A-D.
3. Now, take each solution, A-D, and put it in the middle box of the corresponding Pod Development. Each exercise is labeled with the letter of the corresponding box.
4. Now write four additional solutions around each solution: A-D.
5. After all five worksheets are completed, Identified Problem and A-D, there will be **24 possible solutions** to work with.
6. Transfer the five worksheets, Identified Problem and A-D, to the Final Pod Development, placing the original Identified Problem in the middle box.

An example of this exercise can be found in the Appendix.

Pod Development – Ideation

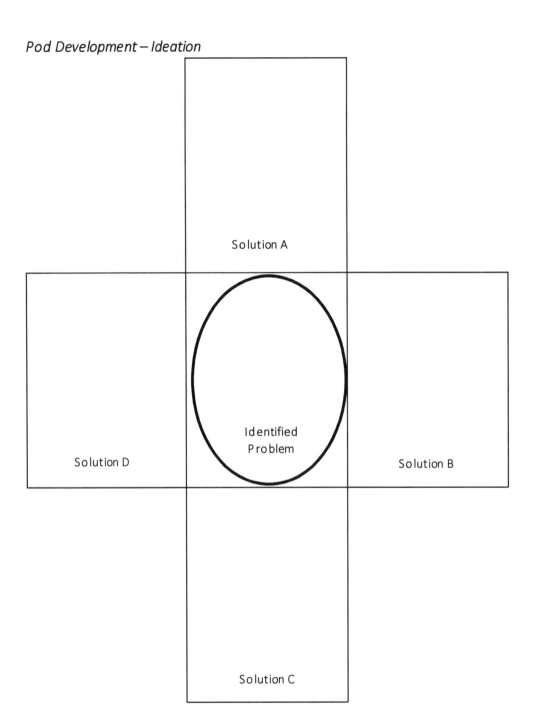

Pod for Solution A

Additional
Solution

Additional
Solution

Solution A

Additional
Solution

Additional
Solution

Pod for Solution B

Additional
Solution

Additional
Solution

Solution B

Additional
Solution

Additional
Solution

Pod for Solution C

Additional
Solution

Additional
Solution

Solution C

Additional
Solution

Additional
Solution

Pod for Solution D

Additional
Solution

Additional
Solution

Solution D

Additional
Solution

Additional
Solution

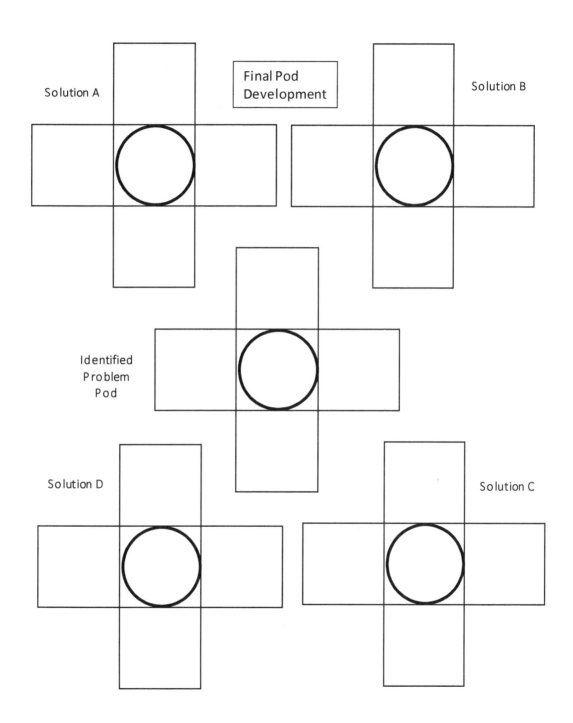

Solution A

Final Pod
Development

Solution B

Identified
Problem
Pod

Solution D

Solution C

Combined Ideation - Ideation Exercise #2

The **combined ideation** is based on gut instincts. While gut decisions may not be fully understood, they are indispensable. With your gut you need to select three solutions that seem to go together. You then need to infer a reasonable way that all three solutions can work in tandem to produce an altogether new idea. Once you combine these three solutions into a new idea that is workable, you will most likely have a potential innovation. The more you work throughout this process, the better you will get at it. Eventually, you reach the point when you can come up with an innovation to most any problem provided that you take the time to work through the ideation process.

Combined Ideation Exercise Instructions:

1. Follow the example on the following page as a guide.
2. Use the Final Pod Development for this exercise.
3. Using your gut instinct, circle three different solutions, or supporting solutions, and place each one in a box in the first ideation/innovation diagram.
4. Force an innovation. Creativity, imagination, and the ability to think deliberately will help create possible innovations.
5. Repeat four times.

An example of this exercise can be found in the Appendix.

Final Pod
Development

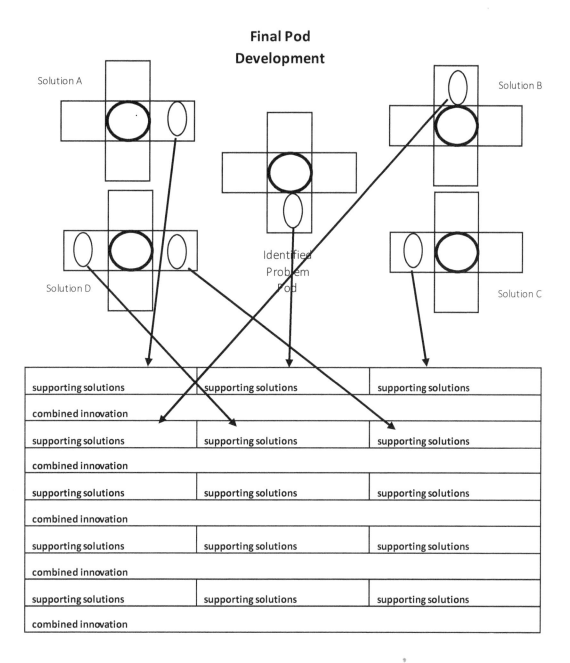

Combined Ideation

Write your problem statement:

supporting solutions	supporting solutions	supporting solutions
combined innovation		

supporting solutions	supporting solutions	supporting solutions
combined innovation		

supporting solutions	supporting solutions	supporting solutions
combined innovation		

supporting solutions	supporting solutions	supporting solutions
combined innovation		

supporting solutions	supporting solutions	supporting solutions
combined innovation		

Combined Ideation Notes

Value Proposition – Ideation Exercise #3

Simon Sinek gives a great TED Talk on how great leaders inspire action. Watch Sinek's talk at https://www.ted.com/talks/simon_sinek. Sinek is a master of understanding value and what it means to the end-user. As you watch the video, consider your value.

Now that you are on the road to innovation, you are going to need to share the message out about that innovation. In other words, you are going to have to tell other people, the end-user, about the value of your innovation. Sinek's talks about starting with *why*. One way to think about the *"why"* of your innovation is to start to compose several belief statements. Once you have your beliefs statements written down, you can step back and craft a statement about the value of your innovation. We call this the *value proposition*.

In the following exercise, consider your beliefs in regard to your innovation. Refer to Sinek's association with beliefs. What do you believe about your innovation and the people who will use it?

An example of this exercise can be found in the Appendix.

Value Proposition

What do you believe about your innovation? If you do not believe in your innovation, why would anyone else? Fill in the boxes.

Write your innovation here:

I believe...

I believe...

I believe...

I believe...

Write your value proposition based on what you believe:

Ideation Input – Ideation Exercises #4 and #5

Now it is time to gather input from people you trust and value. Make sure you choose people who will give you honest feedback. This group of people will be your Advisory Board. Although you may think parents and family members can be brutally honest, some can just be cheerleaders and not want to hurt your feelings. You must be realistic about family members on your board. This is not to say they are bad choices, just use caution. You want honesty!

After you have assembled an Advisory Board, you will invite your board to a meeting. In the meeting you will record minutes to share with your board after the meeting.

Advisory Board

1. Pick at least 5 people who you trust and value their opinions to give you honest feedback for tweaking your innovation.
2. Include at least one **college professor**.
3. Explain what insight, or skill your advisory board member will bring to your innovation.

An example of this exercise can be found in the Appendix.

List 5 people on your advisory board

Write their names, and what they bring to your board

Name:

What does he/she bring?

Name:

What does he/she bring?

Name:

What does he/she bring?

Name:

What does he/she bring?

Name:

What does he/she bring?

Advisory Board Meeting

Now you will need to meet with your advisors in a formal meeting.

1. Determine three areas to be discussed at the meeting. Areas you can include are:
   - Design
   - Advertising
   - Suggested Tweaks
   - Suggested Pivots
   - Possible Funding Sources
   - Users
   - Features
2. Schedule a meeting on your *Outlook* calendar. Check your member's schedule through the "*Scheduling Assistant*" for available times.
   - Using the *Scheduling Assistant* feature assumes your advisors are on campus.
3. Determine time, date, and place of meeting. Face-to-face meetings work best, but Skype works too. You should use *Zoom*, Skype or *FaceTime* for videoconferencing.
4. Take notes during the meeting.
5. After the meeting, transcribe notes to **OneNote**.
6. Share your OneNote file with members and ask them to contribute.
7. Keep your OneNote file as a workable document throughout your innovation.

Tips for holding a great meeting

Ask, don't tell someone to go to your meeting. Have all the information and the requirements of the meeting so an attendee will feel his/her time is valued. Stick to your agenda. Keep everyone involved. Do not do all the talking! Make sure you frequently ask attendees for input during your meeting.

Make sure there is a point to your meeting. Send out your meeting agenda at least one week in advance to give an overview of what the meeting is about. This will help your attendees provide the most helpful information on your innovation.

There is nothing worse than a meeting on Friday afternoon. If your attendees have careers, Friday afternoon is often wind-down time. It is not to say your attendees are trying to skip out early on a Friday afternoon, but most likely they want to finish up some tasks from the week that might have been pushed aside during the rest of the week. Also, most professional brains have worked hard all week, and to heap on an important meeting at the end of the week is not respectful of busy professionals.

Here is a sample agenda outline for your meeting:

Meeting Agenda

Name of Committee: _____

Month, Date, Year: _____

Place of Meeting: _____

Time of meeting: _____

Attendees:

Person 1: _____

Person 2: _____

Person 3: _____

Person 4: _____

Person 5: _____

Committee Objectives:

1. _____

2. _____

3. _____

4. _____

New Business:

1.

2.

3.

Meeting Notes

Looping – Ideation Exercise #6 and #7

Based on your advisory board meeting, will you need to pivot or scale? This is called **looping**. With your meeting information, what do you think? Either direction will need additional ideation.

Now that you have begun executing your innovation, you will likely end up in one of two positions. Perhaps things are going a bit better than you thought and you need to ramp up production to make necessary adjustments. Use the insight you have gained from your advisory board to make needed adjustments.

If your advisory board suggested you have an unmanageable innovation, it might be time to scrap the innovation and start over. Scrapping an innovation is not failure. Scrapping an innovation and starting over takes maturity and insight. Should you ignore the obvious need to scrap your innovation and push it through for the sake of pushing it through, you will end up losing…maybe even resulting in a failure. Don't be that person!

Either situation in which you find yourself is manageable and fixable. You have received new input from your advisory board and other sources, so you will need to loop through the innovation process again. If things are going better than you think, you still have new problems to work through. So, you will need to go back to the beginning of the process and work them through.

If your project has fallen apart, if you want to change to something else, or if it is just underperforming, you are in the same situation of having to start from the beginning. Do not be frustrated; this is rather normal. You have learned and you have discovered how to think systematically. You will begin with *Looping Pod Development* and go through the exercise again with your new direction.

Pivot

A **pivot**, as with a basketball pivot, is when you will remain in the same spot, but you will switch directions. A pivot can be kind of fun because you get to adjust or scrap your innovation to make something better. When you pivot, be sure not to make the same mistakes twice. "Hope springs eternal," and that is especially true in the field of innovation.

As you think through your situation, and a possible pivot, be sure to think deliberately about who might help you and what you might need to do. There is no fault in adding to your advisory board. Innovation does not include limitations in ideation, so think with purpose!

In some instances, circumstances out of your control may make your idea impossible to implement. Since the only correct outcome of an innovation is implementation, in these circumstances you will need to pivot to a new innovation altogether. Do not fool yourself into thinking this is the last time you will have to pivot. Yet, at the same time, do not think that the more pivots you do, the less productive your innovation. That type of thinking is counterproductive, so do not let that seep into your thoughts. Innovation is a process, and pivoting is part of that process.

Once you determine which way to go, pivot or scale, you will complete the Looping Pod and ideate. For some reason, almost all the ideas we think are good are close to what the majority thinks are good ideas as well. If this is the case, a small pivot or change of direction is required so that your larger audience and yourself agree about your innovation's value.

Scale

Scaling is innovation growth. Ask yourself, what can be added to a good innovation to make the innovation better? Depending on your answer, you might scale in a big way, or maybe just a bit.

If a pivot can be fun, scaling is certainly fun. The scale comes after you had some success with your innovation. Now it is time to ramp things up.

Think about what additional resources you will need to enact and enhance your innovation. *Hot Wheels* cars are usually 1:64 scaled. They are one sixty-fourth the size of the real car. They look like the real car but smaller. Your current innovation is a smaller scale of what it will be. It is a baby innovation that needs to grow. The scaling process is thinking through the steps that are necessary to start that process. Do not fool yourself and think that since you are scaling you will not have to pivot in the future.

Looping Pod Development and Looping Ideation instructions:

Depending on your identified direction, pivot or scale, identify the new problem. Put that new problem in the center box of the Looping Pod Development and work through the Looping Pod Development like the original Pod Development exercise. Continue onto the Looping Ideation as you did with your original Ideation exercise.

Looping Pod

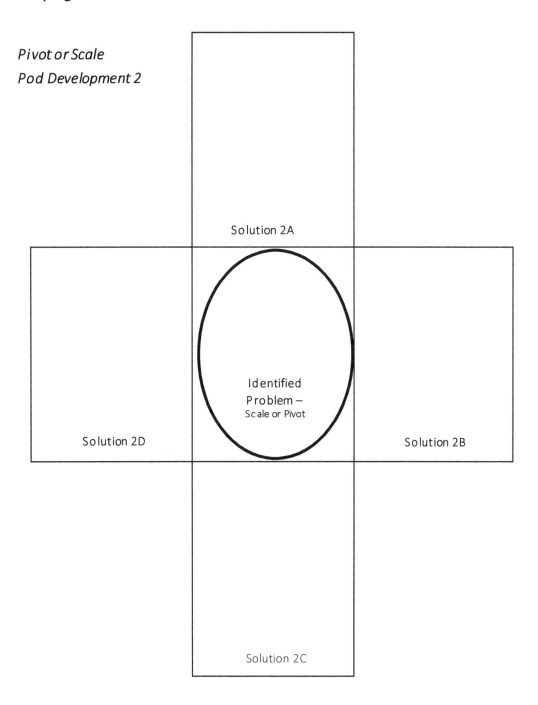

Pivot or Scale
Pod Development 2

Solution 2A

Identified
Problem —
Scale or Pivot

Solution 2D

Solution 2B

Solution 2C

Looping Pod for Solution 2A

Additional Solution

Additional Solution

Solution 2A

Additional Solution

Additional Solution

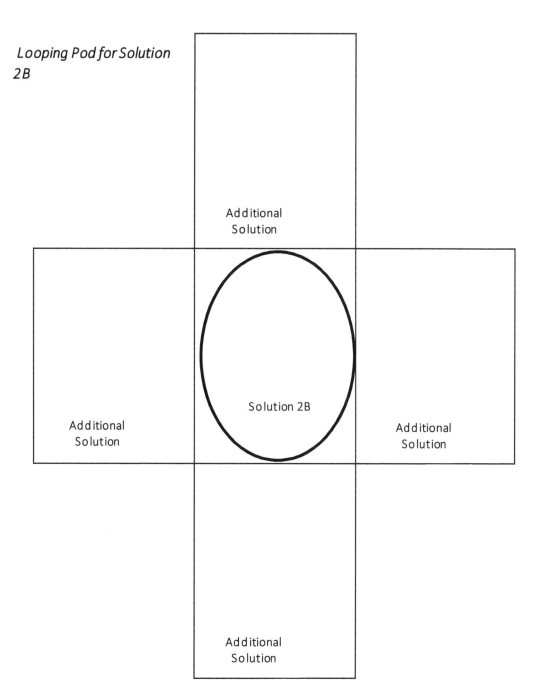

Looping Pod for Solution 2B

Additional Solution

Additional Solution

Solution 2B

Additional Solution

Additional Solution

Looping Pod for Solution 2C

Additional
Solution

Additional
Solution

Solution 2C

Additional
Solution

Additional
Solution

Looping Pod for Solution 2D

Additional
Solution

Solution 2D

Additional
Solution

Additional
Solution

Additional
Solution

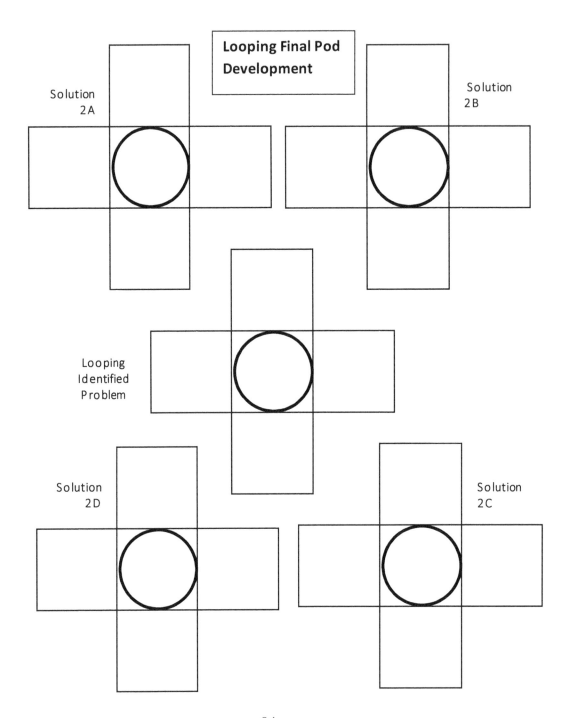

Looping Final Pod
Development

Solution
2A

Solution
2B

Looping
Identified
Problem

Solution
2D

Solution
2C

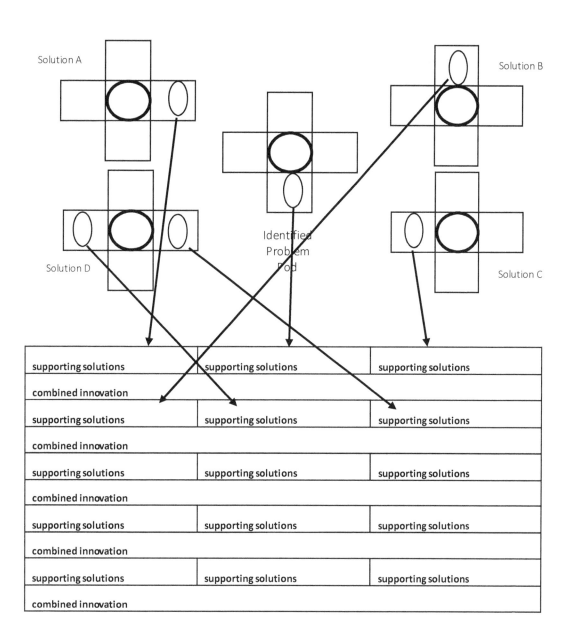

Solution A

Solution B

Identified
Problem
Pod

Solution D

Solution C

supporting solutions	supporting solutions	supporting solutions
combined innovation		
supporting solutions	supporting solutions	supporting solutions
combined innovation		
supporting solutions	supporting solutions	supporting solutions
combined innovation		
supporting solutions	supporting solutions	supporting solutions
combined innovation		
supporting solutions	supporting solutions	supporting solutions
combined innovation		

Looping Ideation

Write your problem statement:

supporting solutions	supporting solutions	supporting solutions
combined innovation		

supporting solutions	supporting solutions	supporting solutions
combined innovation		

supporting solutions	supporting solutions	supporting solutions
combined innovation		

supporting solutions	supporting solutions	supporting solutions
combined innovation		

supporting solutions	supporting solutions	supporting solutions
combined innovation		

Ideation Notes

SMARTER Goals – Ideation Exercise #8

Developing goals helps you organize and evaluate the innovation process.

1. Fill out your SMARTER Goals in the following exercise.
2. Consider your identified possible innovation, then write SMARTER Goals for the organization and execution of your innovation.

What each letter represents:

S is for Specific – be specific enough that if someone was to look at your goal that person could pick it up where you left off and continue the process.

M is for Measurable – is the quantitative part of your goals. Quantitative means numbers. This goal would need to be measured in a quantity. As an example, if you wanted to ask five people for feedback you could judge your goal as a success if you received feedback from all five.

A is for Action – action…in other words, how are you going to get up and make it happen? Stop sitting around and talking about it.

R is for Realistic – being realistic about something is to say you are physically capable of doing it. You can't fly, but you might be able to run or drive.

T is for Time. Set timelines to get things done.

E is for environment - write about who this innovation will affect besides you and your end-user. As an example, if you are a parent, think about how this will affect your children or other people in the same location.

R is for rewards – acknowledge accomplishments with a reward system. What is your reward if you or the end-user accomplishes this goal?

An example of this exercise can be found in the Appendix.

SMARTER Goals

S

M

A

R

T

E

R

Action Plan – Ideation Exercise #9

Watch the following YouTube video on writing action plans:

https://www.youtube.com/watch?v=yx17IXYJgDk

Using your SMARTER Goals, complete the Action Plan exercise. Fill in each column with the following information.

Action Step: Identify five *Action Steps* that need to be completed to implement the innovation.

Timeline: Make a note in the *Timeline* box when the step must be completed. Be specific on the dates, i.e., next Monday or December 10. The chunks of time must be spread out realistically.

Responsibility: Make a note in the *Responsibility* box of who will be responsible for carrying out the action step. This is not always you! Does a friend or family member have a part in your innovation? Write their task down so you can follow up with them to insure your innovation is coming along.

Resources: Make a note in the *Resources* box of what resources will be needed to complete the action step.

Obstacles: Make a note in the *Obstacles* box of possible situations or issues that may arise that will slow down the innovation process.

An example of this exercise can be found in the Appendix.

Action Plan

Action Step	Timeline	Responsibility	Resources	Obstacles
1				
2				
3				
4				
5				

Phase 3
Implementation
Of Your Active Innovation

Class Demo

Peer Evaluation

Tweak Research

Final Implementation Presentation

Peer Evaluation (2)

Self-Evaluation

Implementation

It cannot be stressed enough that innovation is not an innovation until it is implemented, otherwise, it is just an idea. Your innovation presentation must have the ability to be verified. Or it must involve demonstrations or evidence of implementation. In other words, if the class cannot use the innovation, you must bring documentation that someone else did.

Class Demo

The **Class Demo** is your first innovation presentation of your Active Innovation to the class. Although it is assumed you still have work to do, **do not** present an idea. Be sure you are presenting an innovation that can incorporate honest critique. Your demo must be a workable innovation even though change is coming.

Iterative design is the concept that a product does not come out complete. You will present an **alpha-model innovation** to the class knowing that in the next iteration the **beta-model innovation** will be changed for the better. It takes serval iterations to get the product or service just right. This is your first opportunity to find out how to improve on your innovation from peers. This new information will show you what kind of pivot you will need in order to move forward.

Prepare an interactive presentation to demonstrate your innovation's implementation.

You will present in the following format for your class presentation:

3 – 5-minute live presentation with visual props
- Include information gathered from your input sources, and your pivot or scale activity.

Peer Evaluation Form

People enhance their ability to innovate with peer interaction. Listening to presentations is not a passive experience. Listen to the innovations of your peers, and provide three suggestions or alternatives to improve their innovation. Use the following form for peer feedback. After your classmate presents, send a message to the presenter with your feedback.

An example of this exercise can be found in the Appendix.

Presenter's Name:

Your Name:

Innovation presented:

I like the fact that...

I wonder if...

A good next step might be...

Tweak Research

Generational, Gender, and Income Characteristics

The following generations will help you discern the characteristic of certain **demographics.** A demographic is a group of people who share characteristic data. The following demographic categories will help you choose a group or **target market** are: Generations, gender, and earnings.

Generations have very distinct characteristics. The following is a brief outline on generational usage habits.

Silent Generation - 1929-1945

This generation lived through the great depression and are thrifty, modest, no-frills people. New technology, products, and services hold little interest. Most of the Silent Generation is retired, many on fixed incomes.

Baby Boomers - 1946-1964

Are very active and like to impress. Baby-boomers are most likely empty-nesters and have time for entertainment and travel. This generation lived relatively prosperous lives, with low experience in national economic distress. Baby-boomers like to spend money, and many of them have a lot of it. They like to be known for being the first to own something new on the market.

Generation X - 1965-1980

Are less interested in impressing others, but also less interested in achievement – they are considered hard to impress. Gen X children experienced shifting societal values and are also known as the *latchkey kid* generation, as mothers entered the workforce in larger numbers.

Millennials - 1981-1996

Tend to be straight across the board with interest in all areas. Millennials are most interested in cause-based innovations and businesses. They are relationship-based. They are extremely techy, and like the latest in technology.

Generation Z - 1997 to 2010

This generation is mainly still in the educational phase of their life. Student loan debt is of major concern to this generation. As a generation, they have the least amount of belief in the American Dream. They show similar signs toward spending as the Silent Generation, as they experienced the great recession through the experiences of their parents. They are skeptical buyers, and are less likely to be swept up in fads. They are surprisingly frugal youth.

■■

Gender: Males and females have differences in usage habits too. According to the US 2010 Census, both genders tend to be more conservative in all aspects of risk when in a relationship. This includes saving, spending, and trying new things. Sale shopping is more appealing to women than men. Females tend to be shoppers, while males are investors. Females are more communicative in preferences, while males use action to convey their preferences.

■■

Income can be broken up into three categories, low, medium and high. According to the Bureau of Labor Statistics' Consumer Expenditure Survey, lower income earners tend to spend approximately 50% of their income on housing/rent. Based on percentage of income, higher earners (8.2%) spend less on transportation than medium (11.2%) and lower (15.2%). All three income earners cited the following as important: entertainment, including pets and pet care; media equipment and services; admission to events such as movies, sporting events, or plays; and toys for children.

Tweak Research Instructions:

Given the information presented on generations, gender and income, where do you think your innovation will fit? Do the prep work for your Tweak Research by thoughtfully reflecting on who you will be helping besides yourself. Circle the demographics that identify your **target market**. A target market is a group of specific users who will most likely use your innovation.

Now conduct an internet search on the following:

- Research a variety of organizations, listing five organizations that targeted the same market.

- Note five strategies they used to appeal to the target market.

- Now select two strategies that they used to appeal to the target market; and why you chose that strategy.

You will use the information gathered to tweak your innovation to meet the needs of your target market.

An example of this exercise can be found in the Appendix.

Research to Tweak your approach. Choose five organizations that work with the same target market as you:

Prep Work
Identify the target group/market that will use your innovation
Age: teens, 20s, 30s, 40s, 50, 60+
Gender: male, female, both
Income: low, medium, high

Use the guidelines from the demographics, and your prep work and research 5 organizations that cater to the same target market as you.

1.

2.

3.

4.

5.

List 5 innovation strategies that solved their problem.

1.

2.

3.

4.

5.

Choose an innovation or strategy that you can borrow to help your innovation.

Give the reason you chose this:

Choose another innovation or strategy you can borrow to help your innovation.

Give the reason you chose this:

Final Presentation

Now is the time to present your innovation and document your journey. This innovation should reflect input gathered from your peers during your class demo. You will use the following format for your class presentation:

5-minute iMovie presentation

Peer Evaluation

People enhance their ability to innovate with peer interaction. Listening to presentations is not a passive experience. Listen to the innovations of your peers, and provide three suggestions or alternatives to improve the innovation. Use the following form for peer feedback. After your classmate presents, send an email to the presentation presenter.

An example of this exercise can be found in the Appendix.

Presenter's Name:

Your Name:

Innovation presented:

I like the fact that...

I wonder if...

A good next step might be...

Capstone Presentation

Since the entire class has been working on ideas to innovations we need to take your innovation to the next level. By working together, we can all promote each other's work and offer our new thinking to a larger community. You will now present your innovation to a community outside the classroom.

While a mall is a loose affiliation of businesses, our capstone will be mixed with new thinking – you are the new thinkers! This new thinking will be divided up at the capstone by the bucket you identified as your framework.

The academic community will be invited to attend the capstone to see the benefit of your new innovations. The community will have the opportunity to interact with like-minded individuals and to nominate projects for prizes!

For the capstone you will use the presentation you created for your final class presentation or a tweaked version of that earlier presentation if revisions and/or updates were required.

Self-Evaluation

Reflect on your innovation and the journey you took to make it happen. Did you pivot? Did you scale? What did you do well? What could you have done better? Honestly fill out your self-evaluation.

An example of this exercise can be found in the Appendix.

Self-Evaluation

What was it that I wanted to innovate? Refer to your SMARTER Goals.

Date of implementation:	Strategies and pivots used:

Successes:	Failures:

Final outcome:	What would you do differently?

APPENDIX

Exercise Examples

Motivation exercise

Your Intrinsic Motivators

My children
Happiness
Personal achievement
pets

Your Extrinsic Motivators

money
good grades
extra credit

Sleep exercise

Jot down your experience with your sleep exercise in these boxes:

Problem

Having trouble
understanding a math
formula answer

Outcome

Woke up thinking it was an
error in calculation.
Reworked the problem.

Resources exercise

Jot down some of the resources **YOU possess here**

Job on campus
Know how to make an app
Sing
Play the guitar
Good relationship with professors

Jot down some of the resources **YOU have access to**
Professor's knowledge
Parent's money
Girlfriend that can write music
Sister that is in a band

Bucket exercise
See page 40

Bug Report

Bug	Solution
1. trash on campus	start a trash pick up club
2. bullying	start an anti-bullying campaign on campus
3. having to cook when I'm sick	start a cooking delivery service for the sick
4. café food	have a cooking night at the dorm
5. expensive books	do a book exchange
6. getting a dog, but not ready for it	write a blog on dog care
7. being lonely in college	start a devotional blog
8. hair in my face	braiding club
9. not knowing where the parties are	a party locator app
10. friends that bug me while I study	have a study party
11. pesky callers	record a funny saying with friends to play for them
12. cooking in dorm room	create a dorm friendly cookbook
13. ballers with bad habits	a basketball skills camp
14. walking my dog alone	dog walking club
15. long drives home	carpool

Focus Report

Bug: loud dorms
Possible solution: discuss with the RA alternating study times
so there is a time for everyone

(3)

Bug: exercising alone
Possible solution: find dorm mates that like to exercise and set a
schedule

(2)

Bug: expensive textbooks
Possible solution: start a give one get one program for students

(4)

Bug: kids without school supplies
Possible solution: start a supplies drive

(1)

Bug: long lines at Java
Possible solution: make an app for Java

(5)

....

108

Ideate Grid

Pick your favorite **Bug:** kids without school supplies

1
Get my ed majors to go buy supplies for the kids

2
Have the bookstore help. Give a discount to college students that buy and donate a supply for kids

3
Go around the dorm and ask for donations

4
Ask a professor if I can do a supply drive in one of my ed classes

5
Run for office so I can get more money to schools

Peer Evaluation Form

Presenter's Name: Nick

Your Name: Liz

Innovation presented: bookstore partnership supply drive

I like the fact that...

you made it easy for students to contribute. They could buy a supply while buying books.

I wonder if...considered asking the bookstore to purchase extra school supplies.

A good next step might be...asking the education department to help you.

Problem Statement

State your current state:
I have two friends here at school that are in bad relationships

State your current state:
Resources for dating violence

Does Affect

Who? Friends, me, their boyfriends
What? School work, health

Why? No one to talk to

Does Affect

Who? Friends, me, their boyfriends and other without campus help
What? Helps people get help
Why? Live in small town with few resources

Does Affect

Who? People who don't know anyone that is a victim
What? Good relationships

Why? Not in bad relationships

Does Affect

Who? People who don't know anyone in a bad relationship
What? Good relationships

Why? Other resources

Restate: there are people on campus that are in bad relations and don't know what to do

Restate: anonymous resource on campus for people to use if in a violent relationship

Combine the two restates to make a Problem Statement:
There are people in violent relationships here on campus that don't know what to do. If they had an anonymous resource on campus they could get help.

Five Whys of Motivation

Write you final problem from your Problem Statement here: I haven't traveled outside of the US. I would like to travel to other countries.

Why? Why do I want to travel to other countries?

Answer: to explore new places and meet new people

Why? Why do I want to explore new places and meet new people?

Answer: to see the beauty the world has to offer and understand the world and the people in it

Why? Why do I want to understand the world and the people in it?

Answer: To gain and understand different viewpoints of people around the world

Why? Why do I want to understand different viewpoints and gain insight into the world around me?

Answer: To become a more well-rounded individual who doesn't spend his life in one area of the world

Why? Why do I want to become a more well-rounded individual who doesn't spend his whole life in one area of the world?

Answer: To live a more fulfilling, happy life

Root Cause (Motivation): I want to travel to other countries and explore new people and places to become a empathetic individual living a fulfill and happy life while serving others

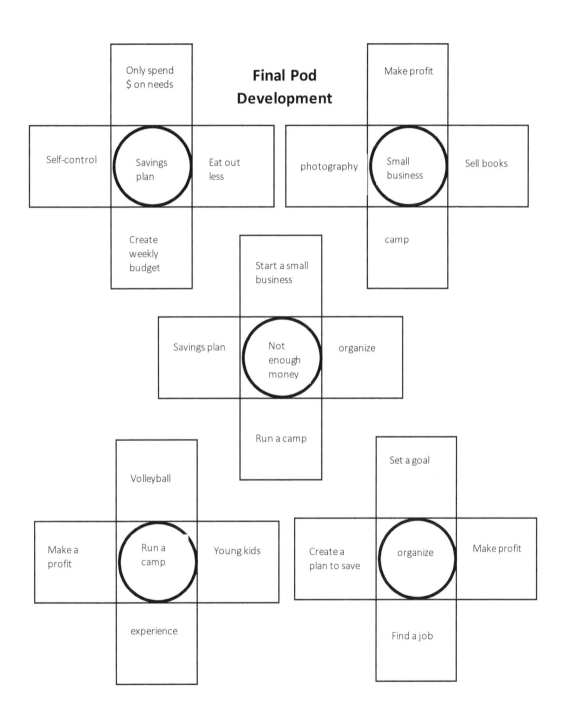

Final Pod Development

Only spend $ on needs

Self-control | Savings plan | Eat out less

Create weekly budget

Make profit

photography | Small business | Sell books

camp

Start a small business

Savings plan | Not enough money | organize

Run a camp

Volleyball

Make a profit | Run a camp | Young kids

experience

Set a goal

Create a plan to save | organize | Make profit

Find a job

Ideation

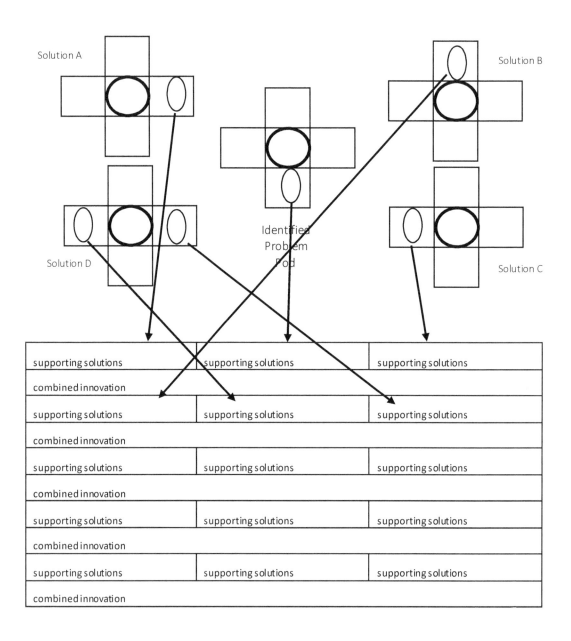

Value Proposition

Write your innovation here: an online group chat for military female fiancés

I believe...there are other girls who have long distant engagement with guys in the military that need someone to understand

I believe... the guys that are stationed together would support the girls having support, even if we were all over the US

I believe...that if we spoke regularly we could talk about upcoming wedding needs and help each other

I believe...this social cause could help both the guys in the military and their fiancés cope with struggles

Write your value proposition based on what you believe: the value of this social cause is to help girls and guys that are in the military that are planning weddings from a distance. The specialty of this group is that we are planning weddings from a distance. The club could help us mentally, spiritually and emotionally.

List 5 people on your advisory board

Write their name, and what they bring to your advisory board

Name: Dr. Digmann

What do they bring? Content knowledge in education

Name: Kaylee

What do they bring? Artistic and creative

Name: Jason

What do they bring? Understands my target market

Name: Dr. Van Horn

What do they bring? Business knowledge

Name: Emma

What do they bring? High school student

Action Steps

Action Step	Time Line	Responsibility	Resources	Obstacles
1 determine cost of socks	Friday	mine	internet	Might be too expensive
2 find sock designs	Sunday	mine	internet	Finding what is "in"
3 order socks	Next Tuesday	mine	internet	Finding best site
4 add design tie dye	Nov. 14	Mine and sister	Go to Walmart	Might not turn out
5 sell on FB page	Nov. 17	Mine and family	Facebook	Finding people to buy them

SMARTER Goals

Write your innovation here: Provide art supplies for students in need.

S	Creating baskets/book bags with art supplies for local students that are in need

M	I will have 4 baskets by Saturday

A	I will need to spread the word. Create a Facebook page

R	Middle of school year because supplies run low

T	I will need to have these made by Christmas break

E	Schools ad student will be effected by this family member will help make them

R	The reward will be helping students in need

Tweak Research

Prep Work
Identify the target group/market that will use your innovation
Age: teens, 20s, 30s, 40s, 50, 60+
Gender: male, female, both
Income: low, medium, high

Use the guidelines from the demographics, and your prep work and research 5 organizations that cater to the same target market as you.

1. Nike

2. DWU Bookstore

3. Amazon

4. Target

5. Boutique

List 5 innovation strategies that solved their problem.

1. design

2. convenience

3. affordable

4. variety

5. style

Choose an innovation or strategy that you can borrow to help your innovation.

Boutique style

Give the reason you chose this:

A lot of girls buy boutique hats

Choose an innovation or strategy that you can borrow to help your innovation.

DWU bookstore convenience

Give the reason you chose this:

People won't buy them if they don't see them around

Self-Evaluation

What was it that I wanted to innovate? Refer to your SMARTER Goals. To start my dorm moving and cleaning service before the end of the semester. To have people who already paid for the service. I have to stay on campus longer than others so I could move their stuff and clean up a bit. So when the maintenance workers come through their dorms will be ready.

Date of implementation:

Dec. 10 to have my list of people

Dec 14 started work

Strategies and pivots used:

Talked to friends in my dorm that leave for Christmas break. Hang flyers, get money in advance.

Successes: I made a lot of money for Christmas

Failures: I had a lot of people use my service. Took longer than expected

Final outcome:

It was successful, I moved and cleaned 10 rooms and made $300

What would you do differently? I would have someone help me.

INDEX

REFERENCES AND RESOURCES

Brain basics: Understanding sleep. (n.d.). Retrieved from National Institution of Neurological Disorders and Stoke website: https://www.ninds.nih.gov/Disorders/Patient-Caregiver-Education/Understanding-Sleep

Chesbrough, H. (2016, May 13). Striving for innovation success in the 21st century. Retrieved from MIT Technology Review website: https://www.technologyreview.com/s/601459/striving-for-innovation-success-in-the-21st-century/

Ellenbogen, J. M. (2005). Cognitive benefits of sleep and their loss due to sleep deprivation. *Department of Neurology, University of Pennsylvania, Philadelphia*, 25-27.

Henderson, S. (**2016, November 3**). Spending habits by generations [Blog post].

Idea generation: Divergent vs. convergent thinking. (2015, April 29). Retrieved from Cleverism website: https://www.cleverism.com/ idea-generation-divergent-vs-convergent-thinking/

Kaufman, J. C., Pumaccahua, T. T., & Holt, R. E. (2013). Personality and creativity in realistic, investigative, artistic, social, and enterprising college majors. *Personality and Individual Differences, 54*(8), 913-917.

Rapattoni, S. (2008). Why create an advisory board? *Financial Executive*, 18.

Razeghi, A. (2008). *The riddle: Where ideas come from and how to have better ones.* San Francisco, CA: Jossey-Bass.

Ringel, M., T, A., & Zablit, H. (2015). The most innovative companies 2015: Four factors that differentiate leaders. *The Boston Consulting Group*, 1-25.

Ryan, R., & Deci, E. (2000). Intrinsic and extrinsic motivations: Classic definitions and new directions. *Contemporary Educational Psychology*, (25), 54-67.

Schneider, J., & Hall, J. (2011). Idea watch: Why most product launches fail. *Harvard Business Review*, 21-23.

Sinek, S. (2009). How great leaders inspire action. Retrieved from TED Talks website: http://www.ted.com/talks

Tjan, A., & Harrington, R. (2012). *Heat, smarts, guts and luck*. Harvard Business Review Press.

UI Experts (Ed.). (2009). What is an action plan? What are the steps to create an action plan? Retrieved from YouTube website: https://www.youtube.com/ watch?v=yx17IXYJgDk

U.S. Department of Education. (2016). *Projections of education statistics to 2016* (National Center for Educational Statistics, Comp.).

Walker, R. M. (2014). Internal and external antecedents of process innovation: review and extension. *Public Management Review*, *16*(1), 21-44.

About the Authors

Dr. Ryan Van Zee, is an Associate Professor of entrepreneurship and the Executive Director of the Kelley Center for Entrepreneurship at Dakota Wesleyan University, in Mitchell South Dakota. He earned his Bachelor of Science degree from Northern State University, a Master of Arts degree from California State University, and a Doctoral Degree from the University of South Dakota.

Van Zee came to DWU with eight years' experience as the director and assistant professor of entrepreneurial studies with the Center for Entrepreneurial Leadership and Innovation at the University of Sioux Falls.

Van Zee received the 2014 Rotary West Presidential Service Award; was a 2013 Autonomous Learning World Caucus Participant from Exeter College, Oxford; a Top 10 finalist for the 2016 South Dakota Governor's Giant Vision Business Plan Competition; and spoke at the 2018 United States Association of Small Business Educator's international conference.

Van Zee is co-author of *The Entrepreneurial Experience: Start Your Business,* with Teresa Quinn.

Teresa Quinn, M.Ed., is a California native with strong family ties to northeastern South Dakota. Quinn served as the Assistant Director of the Kelley Center for Entrepreneurship, and an Assistant Professor of entrepreneurship at Dakota Wesleyan University, in Mitchell South Dakota from 2016-2018. Quinn sat on the Faculty Development Committee and was the CEO Club advisor for the CEO Club chapter at Dakota Wesleyan University, Mitchell.

Quinn holds a Bachelor of Science degree in Small Business Entrepreneurship from California State University, Dominguez Hills, Carson, California, and a Master of Education degree in Sports Management from Northcentral University, Prescott Valley, Arizona. Quinn is finishing her dissertation research for her Ph.D. in Industrial

Organization Psychology from Grand Canyon University, Phoenix, Arizona. Her dissertation research is on student's perceptions of innovation curriculum.

Prior to coming to DWU Quinn worked more than 14 years with the Leona Group, at Desert Hills High School in Gilbert, AZ, and El Dorado High School, in Chandler, AZ, as a teacher in several elective subjects, soccer coach, and the school's athletic director.

Besides her work at DWU, Quinn is co-author of *The Entrepreneurial Experience: Start Your Business,* with Dr. Van Zee, a hobby farmer, successful small-business owner, and mother of three.

CPSIA information can be obtained
at www.ICGtesting.com
Printed in the USA
LVHW011809130819
627499LV00008B/288/P

9 781725 151666